I am feeling

A collection of Islamic prayers and sayings for children

This Book Belongs to:
_____

Compiled by Dr. Mohammed Saleem

Illustrated by Bushra Saleem & Dr. Mohammed Saleem

Copyright © 2021 Universal EDU Enterprises Inc.
All rights reserved.
ISBN: 978-1-7775221-0-0

To my father, thank you for
teaching us the value of prayer.
May Allah have mercy on you and
grant you the highest level of Jannah.

About this book

Emotional intelligence has been suggested as more important than IQ in children's success in life, including academic success. Yet, schools tend to focus primarily on cognitive and social development. EI is usually approached indirectly or becomes part of the reactionary approach to school discipline. School disciplinary policies attempt to help students manage their emotions and feelings; however, they are often reactionary and can also be punitive.

Children are expected to learn aspects of EI implicitly through their family dynamics, social interactions, and in other school and community activities. A proactive approach that enables children to explore their emotions and feelings is often missing. Children must be actively taught emotional literacy, management of emotions, to develop empathy, and intrinsic motivation from a very young age. This is even more important now with mental health becoming a major concern during the COVID-19 pandemic.

Definitions

Emotional intelligence (EI) is the ability to understand and manage our emotions and the ability to understand, and in turn influence, the emotions in other people.

Emotional literacy is the ability to recognize one's own feelings and the feelings of others.

Management of emotions: being able to control one's emotions effectively.

Empathy: Ability to understand and share the feelings of others.

Intrinsic motivation: Pushing oneself to meet one's goals.

This book draws on the rich Islamic heritage to help children explore their feelings and how to manage them effectively. Contrasting feelings are paired to make it easier to differentiate each feeling. Therefore, explore the feelings in pairs. As a way of saying thanks for your purchase, I am providing a companion website with a dedicated page for each feeling containing the following:

- Pronunciation of each prayer or saying
- Videos with detailed explanations for each feeling and the rationale for what to do and say Islamically (watch these videos together with children as you explore each feeling)
- Related resources for each feeling will continue to be added

Please use the link or scan the QR code to visit the website and register your email to access all the videos.

Website: http://bit.ly/i-am-feeling

Table of Contents

I am feeling

1. Happy (Nigeria & Niger)..................8
2. Sad (Nigeria & Niger)....................10
3. Pleased (China)............................12
4. Angry (China)...............................14
5. Thankful (Canada).......................16
6. Wronged (Canada).......................18
7. Kind (Indonesia)...........................20
8. Mean (Indonesia).........................22
9. Loved (Egypt)...............................24
10. Hurt (Egypt)................................26
11. Amazed (Iraq).............................28
12. Bored (Iraq)................................30
13. Innocent (Indian Subcontinent)..32
14. Guilty (Indian Subcontinent).......34
15. Impressed (Yemen).....................36
16. Disappointed (Yemen).................38
17. Blessed (Sudan).........................40
18. Greedy (Sudan)..........................42

19. Brave (Morocco).........................44
20. Scared (Morocco).......................46
21. Content (Saudi Arabia)...............48
22. Jealous (Saudi Arabia)................50
23. Proud (Turkey)............................52
24. Ashamed (Turkey).......................54
25. Humble (Australia)......................56
26. Boastful (Australia).....................58
27. Satisfied (Russia)........................60
28. Frustrated (Russia).....................62
29. Relaxed (Syria)...........................64
30. Tired (Syria)................................66
31. Free (Malaysia)...........................68
32. Trapped (Malaysia).....................70
33. Safe (Kazakhstan).......................72
34. Vulnerable (Kazakhstan).............74
35. Responsible (Tunisia)..................76
36. Careless (Tunisia).......................78

بِسْمِ اللهِ الرَّحْمٰنِ الرَّحِيْمِ

Introduction

Feelings and emotions are universal.

Sometimes we feel happy, like when we are having fun. Sometimes we feel sad, like when someone is mean to us. Sometimes we feel safe, like when we are in the arms of our mother. Sometimes we feel scared, like when a dog is barking at us. Sometimes we laugh, like when someone tells a funny joke. Sometimes we cry, like when we are in pain.

Feelings and emotions are universal. Regardless of where we are from, whether young or old, poor or rich, male or female, nobody can help having feelings and emotions. We go through them daily as different things happen to us. We communicate with each other through our feelings and our emotions. Seeing someone smile, cry, or sad may make us do the same.

What is the difference between feelings and emotions?

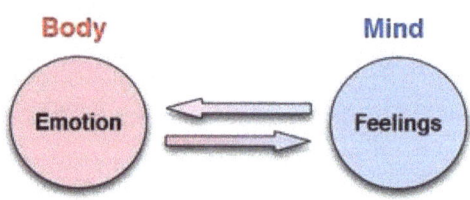

Emotions are physical, whereas feelings are mental. An emotion, like smiling, is a physical response to a change we are experiencing. Feelings and emotions can trigger each other. For example, we may feel tired when we are emotionally drained and physically exhausted or the other way around. Emotions are experienced immediately; whereas feelings develop later after we have gained some more understanding of our emotions.

Different people may feel differently about the same thing.

How we feel about the same thing may differ from person to person depending on our prior experience and culture. We may forget the details of our experiences, but we often remember how we felt during those experiences. Those feelings quickly resurface when we go through similar experiences making us view the same experience in a unique way.

Feelings can cloud our judgement!

We all have feelings, so it is OK to feel happy and sad, pleased and angry, good or bad. What counts is what we do about our feelings. We need to learn to show our feelings in ways that are helpful to us and to others and not in ways that are hurtful.

We often act according to how we feel about things. We may feel more motivated or excited to do something that we enjoy versus something that we do not enjoy. We may be willing to take greater risks if we feel overly excited about something. Acting out in anger can lead to poor decisions. That is why Prophet Muhammad (ﷺ) advised us to control our anger and not to act out in anger.

(Quran 21:107)

Prophet Muhammad (ﷺ) is our role model for managing our feelings.

Prophet Muhammad was sent to a rude and crude people that were shaped by their harsh desert environment; yet, he adopted gentleness over harshness, kindness over meanness, forgiveness over revenge, and love and compassion over hatred and cruelty. Allah reminds us in the Qur'an that Prophet Muhammad was sent as nothing but as a sign of Allah's Mercy to all that exists: *And We have not sent you but as a mercy to the worlds.* (Quran 21:107).

Yet, our beloved Prophet Muhammad was a human being and not an angel. There were times he too would be overcome with conflicting emotions and found it difficult to navigate. But he would regain his composure by turning to Allah. Some of the best examples of this can be found in the prayers and Islamic sayings in the Qur'an and his sunnah. Let us take a closer look at how we can learn to do the same by reflecting on some of these prayers and Islamic sayings. If we make them part of our habits and our character, we will be able to maintain our mental health and live a healthier and happier life.

I am feeling HAPPY!

What makes you happy?

Nigeria and Niger

I am feeling SAD!

What makes you sad?

Nigeria and Niger

I am feeling PLEASED!

What makes you pleased?

China

I am feeling ANGRY!

What makes you angry?

China

I am feeling THANKFUL
towards someone

What makes you feel thankful?

Canada

I am feeling WRONGED
by someone

What makes you feel wronged?

Canada

I am feeling KIND

What makes you feel kind?

20

Indonesia

I am feeling MEAN

What makes you feel mean?

Indonesia

I am feeling LOVED

What makes you feel loved?

24

Egypt

I am feeling HURT

What hurts you?

Egypt

I am feeling AMAZED

What amazes you?

Iraq

I am feeling BORED

What bores you?

Iraq

I am feeling INNOCENT!

What makes you feel innocent?

Indo Subcontinent

I am feeling GUILTY!

What makes you feel guilty?

Indo Subcontinent

I am feeling IMPRESSED

What impresses you?

Yemen

I am feeling DISAPPOINTED

What disappoints you?

Yemen

I am feeling BLESSED

What makes you feel blessed?

40

Sudan

I am feeling GREEDY

What makes you feel greedy?

Sudan

I am feeling BRAVE

What makes you feel brave?

Morocco

I am feeling SCARED

What scares you?

46

Morocco

I am feeling CONTENT

What makes you feel content?

Makkah, Saudi Arabia

I am feeling JEALOUS

What makes you jealous?

50

Madinah, Saudi Arabia

I am feeling PROUD
What make you feel proud?

Turkey

I am feeling ASHAMED
What make you feel ashamed?

Turkey

I am feeling HUMBLE

What makes you feel humble?

Australia

I am feeling BOASTFUL

What makes you boastful?

Australia

I am feeling SATISFIED
What satisfies you?

Russia

I am feeling FRUSTRATED

What frustrates you?

Russia

I am feeling RELAXED
What relaxes you?

Syria

I am feeling TIRED

What tires you?

Syria

I am feeling FREE

What makes you feel free?

Malaysia

When you feel free, say

رَبَّنَا لاَ تُزِغْ قُلُوبَنَا بَعْدَ إِذْ هَدَيْتَنَا وَهَبْ لَنَا مِن لَّدُنكَ رَحْمَةً إِنَّكَ أَنتَ الْوَهَّابُ

Rabbana la tuzigh quloobana ba'ada ith hadaytana wahab lana min ladunka rahmatan innaka anta-lwahhabu

Our Lord! Let not our hearts deviate (from the truth) after You have guided us, and grant us mercy from You. Truly, You are the Bestower.[31]

I am feeling TRAPPED
What makes you feel trapped?

Malaysia

I am feeling SAFE
What makes you feel safe?

Kazakhstan

When you feel safe, say

لاَ إِلَهَ إِلاَّ اللَّهُ وَحْدَهُ لاَ شَرِيكَ لَهُ لَهُ الْمُلْكُ وَلَهُ الْحَمْدُ وَهْوَ عَلَى كُلِّ شَىْءٍ قَدِيرٌ

La ilaha illal-lahu, wahdahu la sharika lahu , lahu-l-mulk wa lahul- hamd , wa huwa 'ala kulli shai'in qadir

None has the right to be worshipped but Allah alone, with no partner or associate. His is the dominion and all praise is to Him, and He is able to do all things.[33]

I am feeling VULNERABLE

What makes you feel vulnerable?

74

Kazakhstan

I am feeling RESPONSIBLE

What makes you feel responsible?

Tunisia

When you feel responsible, say

اللَّهُمَّ إِنِّي أَسْأَلُكَ الْهُدَى وَالتُّقَى وَالْعَفَافَ وَالْغِنَى

Allahumma inni as alukal huda wat tuqa wal afaafa wal ghina

O Allah! I ask You for guidance, piety, safety and well-being, and contentment and sufficiency.[35]

I am feeling CARELESS

What makes you feel careless?

Tunisia

When you feel careless, say

اللَّهُمَّ إِنِي أَعُوذُ بِكَ أَنْ أَضِلَّ أَوْ أُضَلَّ أَوْ أَزِلَّ أَوْ أُزَلَّ ، أَوْ أَظْلِمَ أَوْ أُظْلَمَ أَوْ أَجْهَلَ أَوْ يُجْهَلَ عَلَيَّ

Allaahumma innee aʿoodhu bika an aḍilla aw uḍalla, aw azilla aw uzalla, aw aẓlima aw uẓlama, aw ajhala aw yujhala ʿalayy

O Allah, I seek refuge with You lest I should stray or be led astray, or slip or trip others, or oppress or be oppressed, or behave foolishly or be treated foolishly.[36]

Endnotes

1. Quran, Chapter 1—Al Fatiha, Verse 2
2. Anas ibn Malik (Allah be pleased with him) relates that if any distress befell the Prophet (ﷺ) he would say: يَا حَيُّ يَا قَيُّومُ بِرَحْمَتِكَ أَسْتَغِيثُ O Ever-Living One, O Everlasting One, by your mercy I seek help. Related by Tirmidhi, Sunan (3600)
3. Quran, Chapter 1—Al Fatiha, Verse 2
4. The Messenger of Allah (ﷺ) has said, after seeing two people angry at one another: "I know a word which, if he were to say it, what he feels would go away; he needs to say: أَعُوذُ بِاللهِ مِنَ الشَّيْطَانِ الرَّجِيْمِ I seek refuge in Allah from the cursed devil and all his anger would go away." Sahih Bukhaari, Volume 6, 337
5. The Messenger of Allah (ﷺ) said, "He who is not grateful to the people is not grateful to Allah." Abu Dawud, #4811, The Book of Etiquette, Chapter 11; Tirmidhi, #1955
6. Quran, Chapter 10—Yunus, Verse 85
7. It was narrated that Al-Hasan said: "Aqil bin Abi Talib married a woman from Banu Jusham, and it was said to him: 'May you live in harmony and have many sons.' He said: 'Say what the Messenger of Allah (ﷺ) said: Barak Allahu fikum, wa baraka lakum. (May Allah bless you and bestow blessings upon you.)'". Sunan an-Nasa'i 3371 in-book reference : Book 26, Hadith 176 English translation : Vol. 4, Book 26, Hadith 3373
8. At-Tirmidhi 5/575, Ibn Hibban, Al-Haakim and At-Tabarani; see Sahih At-Tirmidhi 3/184. Source: From the Book "Supplications & Treatment with Ruqyah", Dr. Sa'eed bin Ali Al-Qahtani, Dar-us-Salam Publication
9. Abu Dawud 4/333. Al-Albani graded it good in Sahih Abu Dawud 3/965.
10. Quran, Chapter 2—Al Baqrah, Verse 156
11. Quran, Chapter 3—'Aal Imran, Verse 191; Abu Hurairah (May Allah be pleased with him) reported: The Messenger of Allah (ﷺ) said, "There are two statements that are light for the tongue to remember, heavy in the scales and are dear to the Merciful: 'Subhan-Allahi wa bihamdihi, Subhan-Allahil-Azim.'". Al-Bukhari and Muslim. Arabic/English book reference: Book 16, Hadith 1408
12. Abu Hurairah (May Allah be pleased with him) reported: The Messenger of Allah (ﷺ) said, "There are two statements that are light for the tongue to remember, heavy in the Scales and are dear to the Merciful: 'Subhan-Allahi wa bihamdihi, Subhan-Allahil-Azim'". Ryad Us Saliheen Arabic/English book reference : Book 16, Hadith 1408 (Al-Bukhari and Muslim)
13. Quran, Chapter 3—'Aal Imran, Verse 173
14. Quran, Chapter 3—'Aal Imran, Verses 135-136; Ibn Abbas (RadiyAllahu Anhu) said: The Messenger of Allah (ﷺ) said: "If anyone constantly seeks pardon (from Allah), Allah will appoint for him a way out of every distress and a relief from every anxiety, and will provide sustenance for him from where he expects not." (Abu Dawud)
15. Quran, Chapter 18—Al Kahaf, Verse 39
16. Abu Dawood 5074, An Nasai, Ibn Majah , and #23 in *Al Kalim at Tayyib (The good words)* by Shaykh Al-Islam Ibn Taymiyyah

17. Quran, Chapter 1—Al Fatihah, Verse 2
18. Part of a larger dua narrated by Al-Hakim 1/455 and it was authenticated and agreed by al-Dhahabi, Ibn Khuzaymah 4/218, Ibn Abi Shaybah 4/109, and Al-Bayhaqi in Shu'ab Al-Iman, 4/454, and in Al-Adab No. 1084 and in Al-Da`awat al-Kabir 211, and Ad-Dhiyya Al-Maqdisi in Al-Mukhtara 4/222, and it was classed as hasan by al-Hafiz Ibn Hajar in Al-Futouhat ar-Rabaniyyah 4/383
19. Suleiman, Omar. (2017). What 'Allahu Akbar' really means. Downloaded on 12/30/2020 from https://www.cnn.com/2017/11/01/opinions/allahu-akbar-meaning/index.html
20. Abu Dawud 5095. Book 43, Hadith 323. Grade: Sahih (Al-Albani)
21. Abu Dawud 832. Book 2, Hadith 442. Grade: Hasan (Al-Albani)
22. Sahih Muslim, Hadith 2722
23. Quran, Chapter 11—Hud, Verse 88
24. Quran, Chapter 21—Al Ambiya, Verse 87
25. *Al-Hisn Al-Haseen Min Kalaam Sayyid Al-Mursaleen* by Muhammad bin Al-Jazari
26. Ibn Mas`ud (ra) said: The Messenger of Allah (ﷺ) said, "He who says: *Astaghfir ullah-alladhi la ilaha illa Huwal-Haiyul-Qayyumu, wa atubu ilaihi* his sins will be forgiven even if he should have run away from the battlefield." (Abu Dawud, At-Tirmidhi and Al-Hakim (on conditions of Al-Bukhari and Muslim for accepting Hadith).
27. Ahmad 4/337; 'Amalul-Yam wal-Laylah, p.4; At-Tirmidhi 5/465
28. Prophet Muhammad (ﷺ) said, "Should I not guide to a word from below the Throne, that is from the Treasures of Paradise, Say Lā Hawla wa lā Quwwata illā Billāh ,"لا حول ولاقوة إلا بالله"so Allah will say, My slave has submitted and surrendered himself." [Narrated by al-Hakim, who said it is authentic, and there is nothing in its chain that would weaken it, and al-Dhahabi agreed with him.]
29. Muslim 4/2090
30. Abu Dawood 4/324, Ahmad 5/42, An-Nasaa'i 22/146, Ibn Sunnee 69/35.
31. Quran, Chapter 3—'Aal Imran, Verse 8
32. Quran, Chapter 18—Al Kahaf, Verse 10
33. Bukhari 6403, Book 80, Hadith 98
34. Quran, Chapter 3—'Aal Imran, Verse 173
35. Sahih Muslim 2721
36. Abu Dawud, Ibn Majah, An-Nasa'i, At-Tirmithi. See also Al-Albani, Sahih At-Tirmithi 3/152 and Sahih Ibn Majah 2/336

DR. MOHAMMED SALEEM

Dr. Saleem came as a teenager to the United States and has been involved in Islamic education and the education of Muslim children in North America for the last twenty plus years. A former certified science teacher, he holds a doctorate in Curriculum and Instruction and a Masters in Educational Leadership and a Bachelors in Education. He is married to a loving wife who is also a certified Early Childhood Educator and they have four beautiful children. He currently works as a principal of a full-time Islamic school. He routinely uses Islamic principles to help young children manage their feelings and to maintain their mental health in his role as a father and a school principal.

BUSHRA SALEEM

Bushra is a middle schooler, attending a full-time Islamic school where she is currently memorizing the Qur'an. This is her first illustrated book!

www.ingramcontent.com/pod-product-compliance
Lightning Source LLC
Chambersburg PA
CBHW051258110526
44589CB00025B/2870